Papier-Mâché

BY SUSAN MOXLEY AND JULIET BAWDEN
Written by Juliet Bawden and Diane James
Photography by Jon Barnes

CONTENTS

CWN ™

PRINCETON ■ LONDON

"Papier-mâché" comes from a French word meaning "chewed paper". It is made by building up layers of paper and paste over a mold. When the paste dries, the paper is quite firm and can be painted and varnished.

You do not need any special equipment or tools to make papier-mâché, but all of the things shown here are useful.

Newspaper is particularly good for making papier-mâché, but old wrapping paper or tissue paper can also be used. You can use wallpaper paste, following the instructions on the packet, or make your own paste using the recipes on pages 4 and 5.

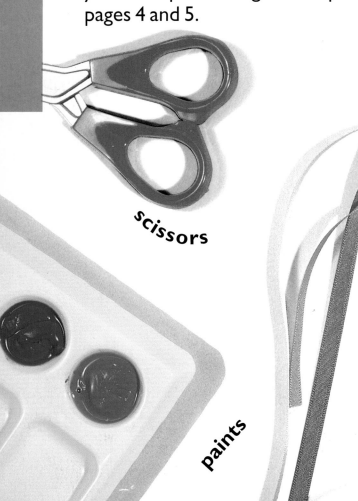

balloons

scissors

ribbons

paints

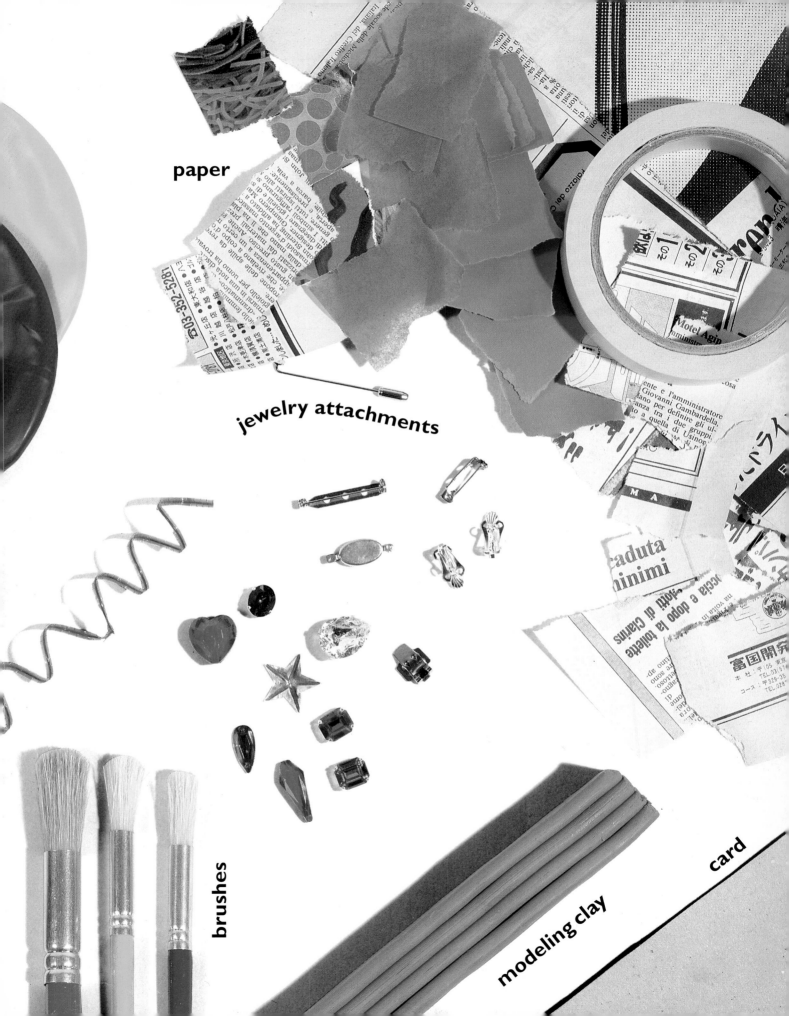

paper

jewelry attachments

brushes

modeling clay

card

There are two methods for making papier-mâché. The first is called "layering", where paste or PVA glue is spread onto strips of paper and several layers are built up over a mold. The second uses pulp. This can be used in the same way as modeling clay to make small shapes.

Making Pulp

Fill a bucket with paper torn into one-inch squares. Pour enough warm water over the paper to cover it and leave to soak for 24 hours. Strain off the water, then gradually add paste or PVA glue until the pulp feels like soft clay.

Wallpaper Paste

Mix according to the instructions on the packet, gradually adding the powder to warm water until it has completely dissolved.

wallpaper paste

pulp

Homemade Paste

Measure out one cup of flour and three cups of water. In a saucepan, mix the flour with a little of the water to make a smooth paste. Add the rest of the water and ask a grown-up to heat the mixture until it boils, stirring all the time! When it is boiling, turn the heat down and let the mixture simmer until the paste thickens. Leave the mixture until it is cold.

Layering

You can rip paper into long strips and spread paste onto each strip as you work. Or spread the paste onto a large sheet of paper. Rip the paper in half lengthways. Stick one piece on top of the other so that both pieces are glue side up. Repeat this so that you have four layers. Paste these over your mold.

layering

homemade paste

You can make bowls, vases, and jugs by using molds such as balloons, large bottles, and cake tins. First, cover the mold with oil or Vaseline™ so that you can pull off the papier-mâché object easily when it is finished. You will need at least six layers of papier-mâché to make a firm shape. Let the shape dry thoroughly before removing the mold. This may take two or three days.

Leave the rim uneven or neaten it by gluing overlapping strips of paper around it. You can also trim the edge by carefully cutting around it with scissors.

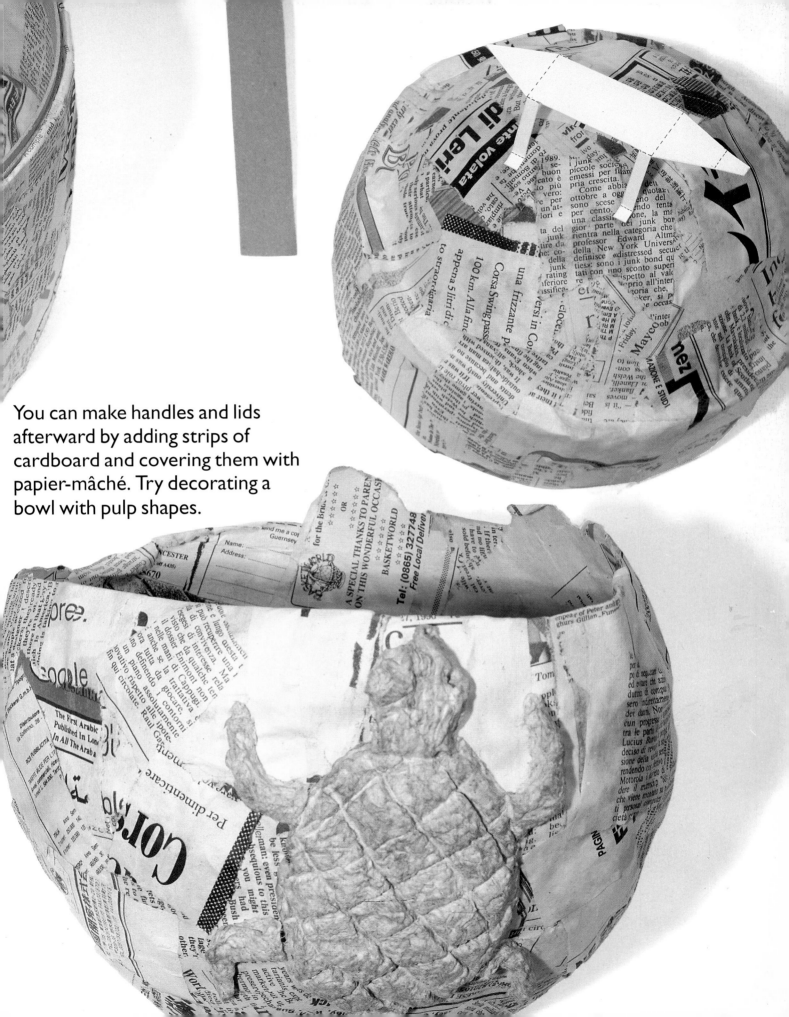

You can make handles and lids afterward by adding strips of cardboard and covering them with papier-mâché. Try decorating a bowl with pulp shapes.

When your papier-mâché objects are completely dry – usually after two or three days – you can decorate them with paint or colored paper. If you have used newspaper, it is a good idea to cover the object with a base coat of white emulsion paint.

After you have decorated the papier-mâché, you can protect it with a final coat of varnish. Watered-down PVA glue can also be used. If you want your papier-mâché to be waterproof, use two or three layers of varnish.

To make a circular bowl stand up, you will have to give it a base. The bowl above has conical feet made by taping cardboard cones to the bowl before decorating.

Here are some toys to make from papier-mâché. We made the cat using an empty bottle of dishwasher liquid as a mold. For the others, we made our own molds using a small balloon, wire, cardboard, and pantyhose for stuffing! Try making a simple shape from card, paper, and Scotch™ tape. Cover your shape with layers of papier-mâché. It does not matter if you cannot remove the finished papier-mâché shape from the mold.

Bird
Crumple a large ball of paper for the body. Use a cardboard roll for the neck and a ball of paper for the head. Add a small cardboard cone for the beak. Tape wire legs to the body. Cover the whole bird in layers of papier-mâché. When it is dry, paint in bright colors.

Russian Dolls
Start with a mold made from an egg-shaped piece of modeling clay. Cover with layers of papier-mâché. When the papier-mâché is dry, cut through it about three-quarters of the way up. To keep the two pieces together, make a ring from a thin strip of cardboard and tape it inside the bottom half. Make lots of different-sized dolls to fit inside one another.

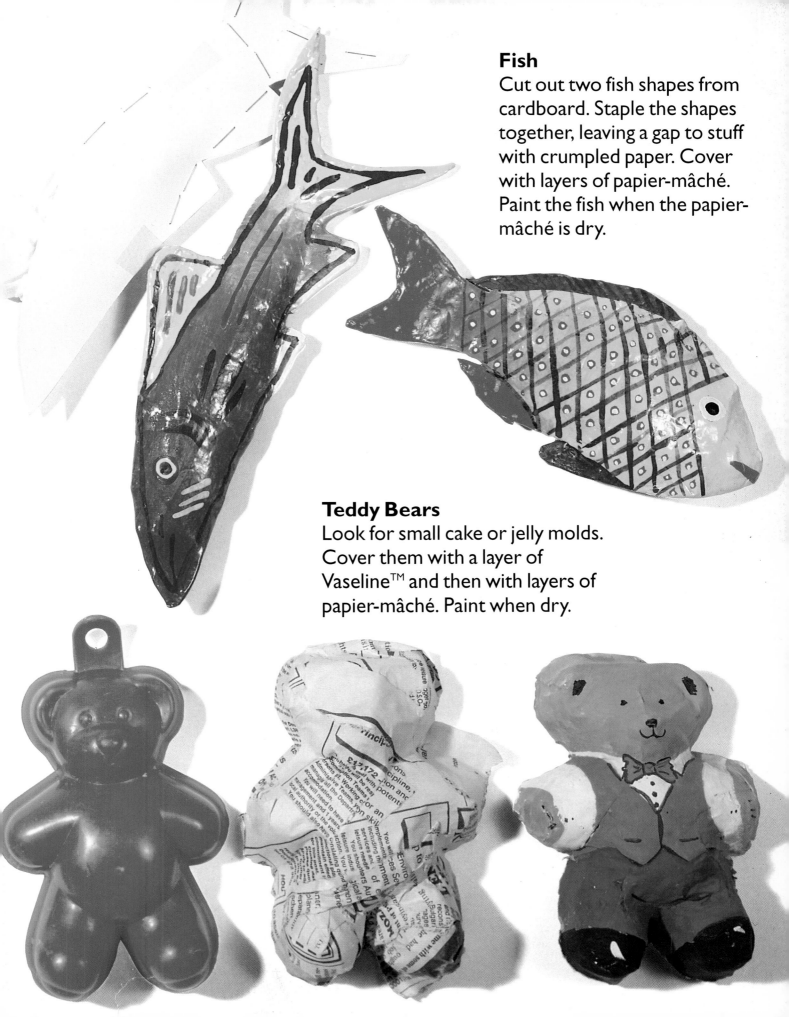

Fish
Cut out two fish shapes from cardboard. Staple the shapes together, leaving a gap to stuff with crumpled paper. Cover with layers of papier-mâché. Paint the fish when the papier-mâché is dry.

Teddy Bears
Look for small cake or jelly molds. Cover them with a layer of Vaseline™ and then with layers of papier-mâché. Paint when dry.

All of this wonderful jewelry is made from papier-mâché! The golden "jewels" were made from paper pulp. You can buy jewelry fittings, such as pin backs and earring clips, from craft stores.

Bows
Paste several strips of newspaper together. Fold each end into the middle to make a bow shape. Paste a thin strip of paper around the middle of the bow.

Earrings
Cut shapes from cardboard and tape on some crumpled paper as padding. Cover the cardboard and paper with layers of paste and paper. Decorate your earrings and glue on earring backs.

Beads
You can make simple beads by winding strips of pasted paper around a straw or pencil. Leave to dry before decorating and threading them. Beads can also be made from pulp (see recipe on page 4). Mold the pulp into shapes and make a hole with a knitting needle. Or push in paper clips to make links.

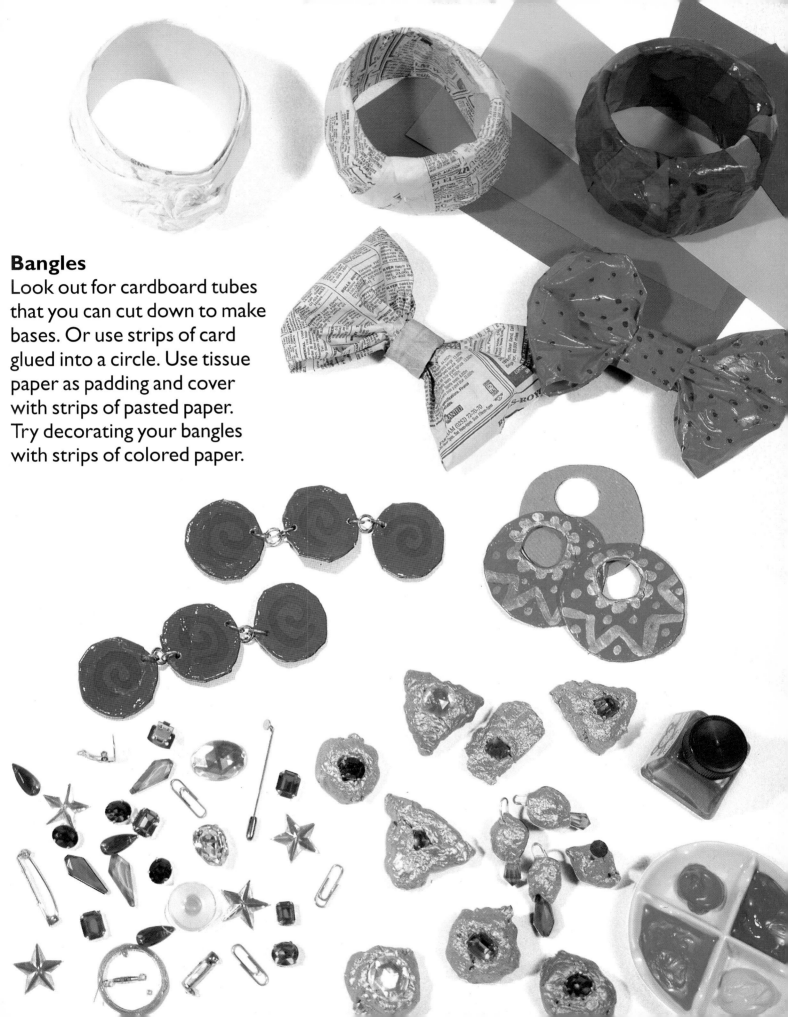

Bangles
Look out for cardboard tubes that you can cut down to make bases. Or use strips of card glued into a circle. Use tissue paper as padding and cover with strips of pasted paper. Try decorating your bangles with strips of colored paper.

You can even make exotic hats with papier-mâché. Round cake tins make good molds for simple hats. Or you could use a balloon to make a rounded top and then add a cardboard brim.

Try decorating your hats with papier-mâché flowers and animals. Or use paper pulp to make brightly colored jewels.

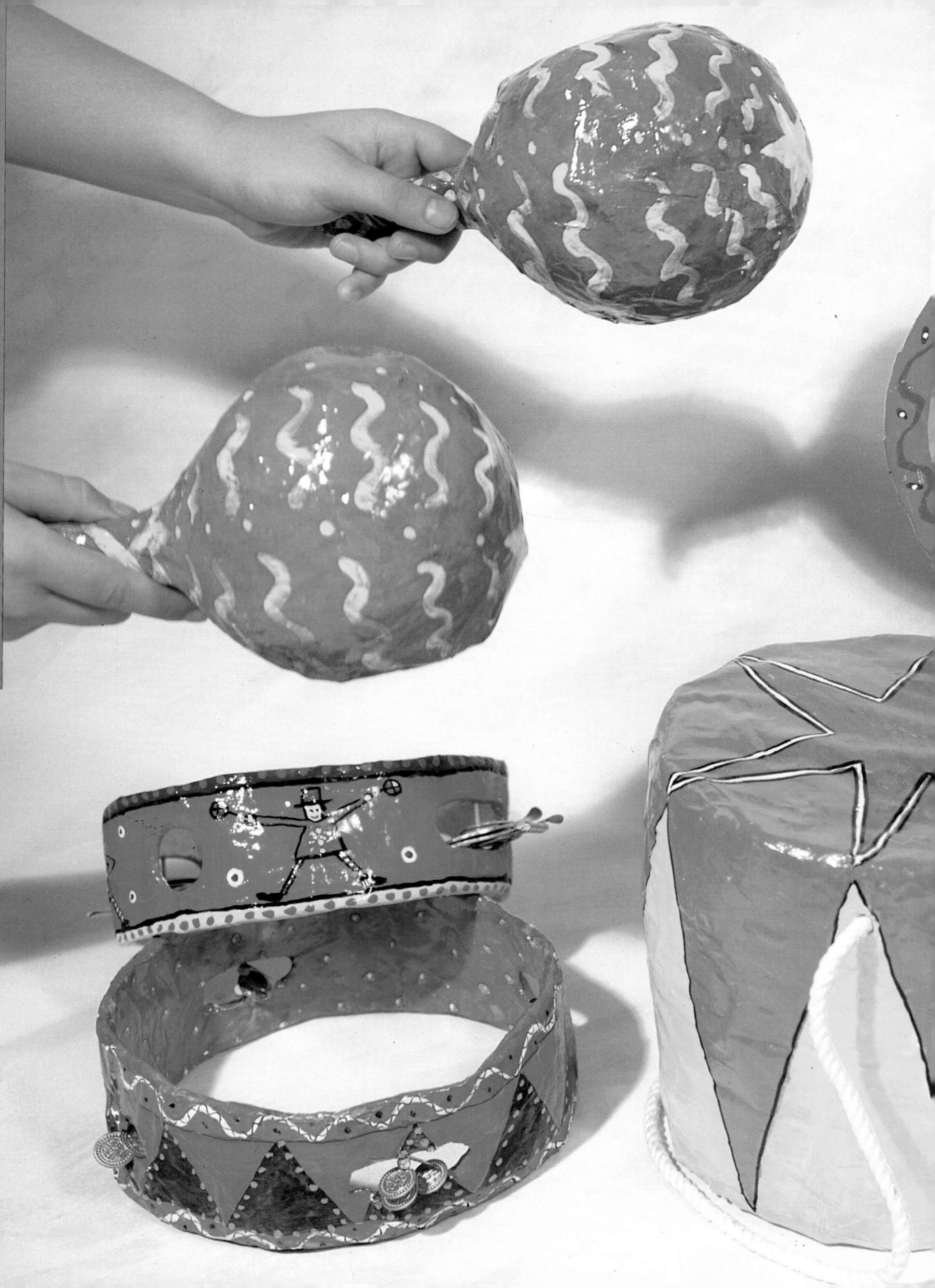

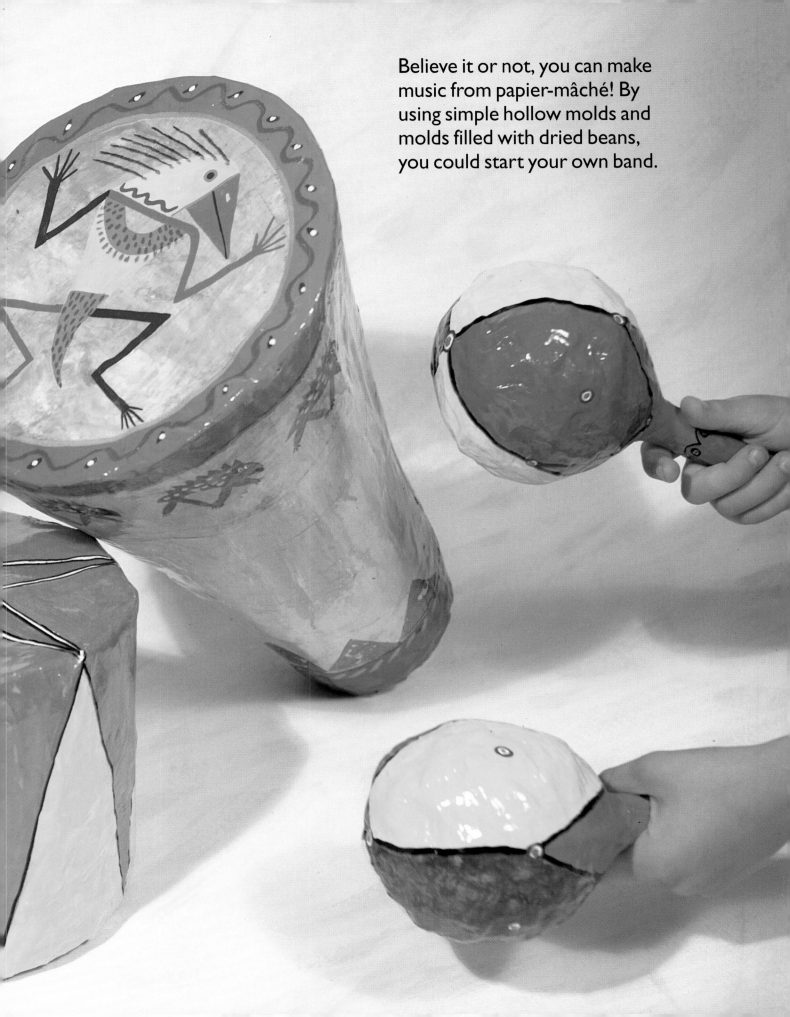

Believe it or not, you can make music from papier-mâché! By using simple hollow molds and molds filled with dried beans, you could start your own band.

Drum

Use a cake tin as a mold, and make two papier-mâché sections like the ones shown here. Cut two holes in the top section and thread some cord through. Join the sections together with strips of pasted paper. When the drum is dry, decorate it with bright colors.

Tambourine

Make a band from cardboard and cut four wide slits in it. Thread beads, washers, or bottle tops onto toothpicks and tape these in the center of each slit. Cover the band with layers of papier-mâché and decorate.

Maracas

Cover a small balloon with papier-mâché, leaving a hole at one end. Fill with dried peas or beans, and seal the hole. Add a handle and decorate.

Papier-mâché has been used for hundreds of years to make puppets. Countries all over the world have their own traditional designs.

Try making glove, spoon, or finger puppets from papier-mâché. You will find some helpful hints on the next page. You could also make a simple stage and give your own puppet show!

Glove Puppet

Make a simple head shape from crumpled paper. Attach it to a neck made from a circle of cardboard. Add features such as ears and a nose and cover with papier-mâché. Paint on other features when the head is dry.

Cut two rectangles from pieces of fabric and stitch together to make the body. Remember to leave holes for your fingers and a hole to push the card tube through. Decorate with ribbons, buttons, or beads.

Finger Puppets

Make a roll of cardboard to fit around your finger. You can add a head made from crumpled paper, and a beak or ears made from card cones, or a hat with a brim. Cover the shape with papier-mâché and decorate it when it is dry. Try making a different puppet for each finger.

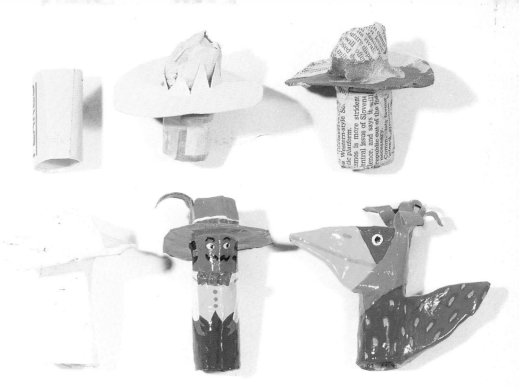

Spoon Puppet

Wrap layers of paper around the top of a wooden spoon to make a head shape. Cover with layers of papier-mâché. Tie a length of dowel to the spoon handle under the head to make a "T" shape. Make the body by sewing two rectangles of fabric together and fitting over the "T" shape.

Masks are great fun for parties, especially if you don't want anyone to recognize you! You can make exciting masks from papier-mâché, and they can be used over and over again.

Many countries have traditional masks that are worn for festivals. You may be able to find inspiration by looking at examples in books and museums.

One of the simplest ways to make a mask is to half cover a balloon with papier-mâché. You can add cardboard cones, sections from packaging, or pieces of crumpled paper to make extra features.

Make holes on either side of the mask and attach string or ribbons to tie around your head. Don't forget to make holes for the eyes.